SIGNS OF THE
SEASONS

Signs of
Summer

Paul Humphrey

Photography by Chris Fairclough

**W
FRANKLIN WATTS**
LONDON • SYDNEY

© 2001 Franklin Watts

First published in Great Britain by
Franklin Watts
96 Leonard Street
London
EC2A 4XD

Franklin Watts Australia
56 O'Riordan Street
Alexandria
NSW 2015

ISBN: 0 7496 4037 5
Dewey Decimal Classification 574.5
A CIP catalogue record for this book is available from the British Library

Printed in Hong Kong/China

Planning and production by Discovery Books
Editors: Tamsin Osler, Kate Banham
Design: Ian Winton
Art Director: Jonathan Hair

Photographs:
Bruce Coleman: 12 (Dr Frieder Sauer), 13 (Sandro Prato), 15 top (Kim Taylor),
16 (George McCarthy), 19 (Kim Taylor); Papilio photography 17;
Discovery Picture Library: 23.
All other photography by Chris Fairclough.

'Sticky Licky' from *Smile Please!* by Tony Bradman © 1987.
Reproduced by permission of Penguin Books Ltd.

CONTENTS

Summer is coming.
Look for the signs of summer.

In summer, the weather is warm.

Sometimes you have to stay in the shade.

You can go to the beach...

...or go out for a picnic.

Gardens are full of flowers in summer...

...and the trees are covered in leaves.

Bees feed on
the flowers.

They take pollen and nectar
back to their hives.

13

Thirsty plants need water.

The birds need a
drink, too...

...and so do you.

15

Lizards warm up
in the sunshine…

...and so do butterflies.

17

There are lots of
caterpillars in the
garden.

The birds like to
eat them.

In summer you can go for a bike ride...

20

...or play cricket.

You can cool down in the paddling pool...

...or eat an ice-lolly.

There are lovely ripe
strawberries…

...and fresh, home-grown vegetables.

In summer it stays light and warm
until late in the evening.

You can have a barbecue!

What other signs of summer can you see?

Sticky Licky

In the summer,
When it's sunny,
Eating ice-cream
Can be funny.

Ice-cream melts
And drips so fast
It's quite hard
To make it last.

It's so lovely,
Sweet and licky,
But when it drips,
You get sticky.

I get ice-cream
On my clothes,
In my hair
And up my nose.

My dad says
I should eat less;
Ice-cream plus me
Equals - mess!

Tony Bradman

INDEX